The Discussion

The Discussion

Conversations Among the Family

Irlean Craven

iUniverse, Inc.
New York   Bloomington

The Discussion

Conversations Among the Family

Copyright © 2009 by Irlean Craven

iUniverse books may be ordered through booksellers or by contacting:

iUniverse
1663 Liberty Drive
Bloomington, IN 47403
www.iuniverse.com
1-800-Authors (1-800-288-4677)

ISBN: 978-1-4401-7679-1 (pbk)
ISBN: 978-1-4401-7680-7 (ebk)
ISBN: 978-1-4401-7681-4 (hbk)

Printed in the United States of America

iUniverse rev. date: 12/09/2009

Contents

Participants

Uncle Evan (Bear): He is very emotional about his opinions and often roars like a bear when he makes an effort to convince another person that his opinion is the truth. He has issues with women and often uses his bearlike tactics to intimidate women.

Auntie Iris: She uses kindness to kill. She will give you a very wonderful story that has a lot of meaning, but, at the end of these insightful stories, lays her power. Upon breaking you down mentally, she will invoke her feelings through her words and cause her subjects to squirm in discomfort.

Steve (General): He plays no games when it comes to letting the truth go. He has little or no remorse for expressing the truth of the matter, especially when it comes to addressing the hypocrisies of the Bear's lifestyle. By the way, he's young and sexy.

Auntie Teresa: She loves Jesus and nothing else. If you cannot talk to her about uplifting the name of Jesus, then she will give you and your foolishness a small corner of her time.

Dee Dee (Soldier): She is the most opinionated of the bunch. She loves to shout and smile about whatever the topic may be, and she can sting you with her sharp remarks. She's very passionate about standing for the truth and exposing corruption within the political arena. It's very difficult to get the soldier to give up. She has also been referred to as a "moving target."

Uncle Roger (Bible Thumper): He goes to church all the time and is on guard 24-7 against the enemy, the devil. When talking to him, it's very important you keep everything in perspective. Failure to do so will cause his Bible's heavy hand to go buck wild.

Tracy: She is a firm believer in the promises of God. She always shines the light on darkness and points out the devil(s) in the midst. She is rarely the center of confusion and is great at silencing the phony saints.

Monica: She is very smart and witty. She is the ninja warrior. Alone in a world of her own and forced to interact with the foolishness of others, she often reacts in a cold-natured way in an effort to let her subjects know she isn't into entertaining foolishness. She can cut you with the truth and not even blink.

Foxxy: She is the comical yet serious one. She has a great understanding of biblical knowledge and loves to provide her creative insight on matters. The only time she will cease with displaying her flamboyant personality is if you start giving high regards to false doctrine. Then she transforms into Wonder Woman and will begin fighting for Jesus.

Therefore I endure everything for the sake of the elect, that they too may obtain the salvation that is in Christ Jesus, with eternal glory.

2 Timothy 2:10

Chapter One

Do You Really Understand the Plan of Salvation?

Irlean Craven

From: Evan

To: Family

Steve and I have been discussing what the term "saved" is according to the Bible. I say it is being born again of the water (baptism) and of the Spirit, that is, the spirit of God or the Holy Spirit. I would like everyone to read the following Scriptures and let me know what you think: Acts 2:38 and John 3:5. My understanding is straight from the Bible. Water baptism is part of the plan of salvation, straight from Jesus' mouth, John the Baptist, and Peter the Rock. What is your understanding? Please make sure you send me Scriptures. Also, please answer these questions. Did Jesus and his disciples baptize people in water? If so, what is the Scripture that verifies this? I know the answer to this question. I just want to know if you do.

John 3:5–7 says:

There was a man of the Pharisees, named Nicodemus, a ruler of the Jews: The same came to Jesus by night, and said unto him, "Rabbi, we know that thou art a teacher come from God: for no man can do these miracles that thou doest, except God be with him." Jesus answered and said unto him, "Verily, verily, I say unto thee, Except a man be born again, he cannot see the kingdom of God." Nicodemus saith unto him, "How can a man be born when he is old? Can he enter the second time into his mother's womb, and be born?" Jesus answered, "Verily, verily, I say unto thee, Except a man be born of water and of the Spirit, he cannot enter into the kingdom of God." That which is born of the flesh is flesh; and that which is born of the Spirit is spirit. Marvel not that I said unto thee, Ye must be born again.

Acts 2:38–40 says:

Then Peter said unto them, Repent, and be baptized every one of you in the name of Jesus Christ for the remission of sins, and ye shall receive the gift of the Holy Ghost. For the promise is unto you, and to your children, and to all that are afar off, even as many as the Lord our God shall call. And with many other words did he testify and exhort, saying, Save yourselves from this untoward generation.

Irlean Craven

From: Monica

To: Family

My understanding of salvation is simple. It is not through water, and it is not the Holy Spirit. Salvation is being saved from the pits of hell. And, in order to do this, you must believe in your heart and confess with your mouth that God raised Jesus from the dead. And you shall be saved. It's just that simple.

Romans 10:9–10 says:

That if you confess with your mouth, "Jesus is Lord," and believe in your heart that God raised him from the dead, you will be saved. For it is with your heart that you believe and are justified, and it is with your mouth that you confess and are saved. Not water and not through the acceptance of the Holy Spirit. The water baptism is symbolic of who you belong to, not evidence that you are saved. The Holy Spirit is sent to dwell within you after you have been saved. You cannot receive the Holy Spirit until after you have been saved.

Salvation is truly between you and God. That's what I believe.

From: Evan

To: Monica

Thanks for your response. I knew you would not be scared to respond. Now, in 2 Cor 13:1, the Bible says let every word be established by two or more witnesses. "This is the third time I am coming to you. In the mouth of two or three witnesses shall every word be established." I have John, Jesus, and Peter as my witness to the plan of salvation being repentance, water baptism, and then baptism by the Holy Spirit. I have given you the Scriptures from all three people already. Please give me more than one Scripture (from one person, Paul) to establish your belief.

Irlean Craven

From: Evan

To: Monica

How do you reconcile what Paul says with what Jesus said? If Jesus said you must be born again of the water and the Spirit, then who trumps who? I say Jesus trumps Paul. I believe Paul was simply trying to get people to take the first step in being saved, believing in God. Then God sent his son Jesus to die for our sins, and Jesus is Lord.

I thought I would add this additional comment. Remember, Paul is the one you are quoting in the book of Romans. Paul was the one who said let every word be established by two or three witnesses.

From: Evan

To: Monica

Read Matt 28:19.this scripture out of the survival scroll (The Bible):

Matthew Chapter 28 verse 19

"19": "Go ye therefore, and teach all nations, baptizing them in the name of the Father, and of the Son, and of the Holy Ghost." Why did Jesus keep telling us to be baptized if it was not his purpose to instruct everyone to be baptized in water and the spirit of God?

Irlean Craven

From: Evan

To: Monica

Read Mark 16:15–18, where Jesus told everyone to go into all the world and preach the gospel to every creature.

> And he said unto them, "Go ye into all the world, and preach the gospel to every creature. He that believeth and is baptized shall be saved; but he that believeth not shall be damned. And these signs shall follow them that believe; In my name shall they cast out devils; they shall speak with new tongues; They shall take up serpents; and if they drink any deadly thing, it shall not hurt them; they shall lay hands on the sick, and they shall recover."

It is important to have the sign of speaking in tongues as well. I'm not talking about prophesying in tongues. I'm referring to speaking in tongues to demonstrate the spirit of God is in you.

From: Monica

To: Evan and Tracy

I had to meditate on what is was to be born again. The Scripture states that one must be born again to see the kingdom of God. Right? I believe that being born again is a state of being. Nicodemus said, "How can one be born again when he is old?" Because you cannot reenter into the womb again, this has to be a state of believing. To be made new is to allow God to be the Lord of your life and allow him to have control over your life instead of you making choices for yourself. You are saying, "Lord, I give up and help me." It acknowledging that God is in charge and you are not. It's a rebirth. Old things have passed away. Behold all things are new. You are a new creature in Christ. This is my understanding of what it is to be born again.

But you cannot be born again until you receive salvation, which is by confessing and believing. Once this is done, then (and only then) can you be born again. The change takes place. It is through this salvation, that is, confessing and believing, that you allow God into your life to change you. Once you are saved, you are born again and therefore allowed to see the kingdom of God. I still believe that water baptism is a symbolic expression for humans to show who you belong to. No other religion but Christianity baptizes. I believe you can be saved and never be baptized because the Scripture states I am saved through confession and believing. I will still see the kingdom of God.

John 3:5 says, "No one can enter the kingdom of God unless he is born of water and the Spirit." "Born of water and the Spirit" can be understood in various ways.

- It means much the same as "born of the Spirit."

- Water here refers to purification.

- Water refers to baptism of John or Jesus and his disciples.

- Water refers to physical birth, specifically to the water of the amniotic sac.

Regarding the Scripture you attached about the Holy Spirit, this is so the Holy Spirit may dwell in you. Every one of you must repent, that is, ask for forgiveness, so you may receive the gift of the Holy Spirit. God and the devil cannot dwell in the same place. If you are sinning and living a life of sin, you need to repent about that so the Holy Spirit may dwell within you and provide you with comfort. Once again, you cannot receive the gift of the Holy Spirit until after you have confessed and believed, which results in salvation. This Scripture talks about how the men of Israel felt guilty for what they believed and behaved. Peter told them to repent and be baptized. These are just my thoughts.

From: Evan

To: Monica,

Steve and Dee Dee, because I have not received any responses from either of you regarding the plan of salvation, which Jesus, John the Baptist, and Peter laid out for all of us to follow, I assume you are just scared to respond because of your position on the issue. Baptism is not required, according to Steve. I have given verse after verse from the Bible, where Jesus says, "Be baptized by the water and the Spirit." Steve, I know this cuts your heart, but give in to the word of God. The Bible says we should let God be the truth and every man a liar.

John 4:1–3 states Jesus had his disciples baptizing people after John the Baptist baptized Jesus. Pay attention to the first two verses. If you don't, you will read right past it and not get what it is saying.

Irlean Craven

From: Steve

To: Evan

I want you to read Genesis and Revelations and all the books in between.

From: Evan

To: Steve

You are not funny!

Irlean Craven

From: Evan

To: Monica

But how do you reconcile the actual, literal baptism of Jesus and he later saying to Nicodemus that he must be born again of the water and the Spirit? Explain that to us.

It is good you have the other meanings for baptism in water and the Holy Spirit, but Jesus, Peter, and John the Baptist were literally submerging people in water (Jordan River) for the water baptism. Peter literally spoke in other tongues (the day of Pentecost in the upper room) as evidence of receiving the Holy Spirit. So what do you have to say about the literal events that happened according to the biblical Scripture? Please reconcile this for us.

From: Dee Dee

To: Evan and Monica

Remember, Evan, Jesus said man is born of water and the Spirit. The first birth is by water; the second birth is by the Holy Spirit. Do not get it twisted. Follow the conversation, not your interpretation of the conversation, please!

Irlean Craven

From: Dee Dee

To: Evan and Monica

First, Evan, make sure you are getting what Jesus Christ said right before you imply that Paul was out of order, okay?

From: Dee Dee

To: Evan

Jesus did not say to Nicodemus that he had to be born of water. Jesus said that man was born of water first. Then his spirit must be born again by the Holy Spirit. Please read it again slowly this time.

Irlean Craven

From: Dee Dee

To: Evan

John 4:1–3 states clearly that, though Jesus baptized not, his disciples did. Remember the Pharisees heard that Jesus Christ had baptized more people that John, but Jesus had baptized not. His disciples did. Who is paying you to be this stupid? Can you read the Scriptures aloud to yourself and follow the thought?

From: Evan

To: Dee Dee

You must not have read what I said. In your zeal to try to make me be "stupid," as you say, you are the stupid one. The fact is:

- Jesus was baptized.

- Jesus had his disciples baptize others.

- Peter told everyone to be baptized as part of the plan of salvation.

So those who believe baptism is not necessary need to read for themselves, and let God reveal the truth to them on their own level. I am not trying to convince anyone. I'm just trying to give you the Scripture where two or more have agreed on what the truth is.

Let me say it to you again. The Bible states that Jesus had his disciples baptizing people after John the Baptist baptized Jesus. Do you think his disciples would have been doing anything if Jesus did not command them to do it? Of course not. Does the boss have to do the job, or does the boss tell his workers to do the job and then manage them? Of course, the boss manages the workers, but the workers only do what the boss tells them to do. Now do you understand?

Who is paying you to be so stupid? You cannot even take the time to read what I wrote to you. I can tell this is why you did not want to respond to the question prior to me sending out the answer. You wanted to be able to get a jab in. Well, you missed me!

Remember to stay focused on the subject here. Jesus had his disciples baptize people. Jesus was baptized himself. John the Baptist baptized people in water. Peter told everyone to be baptized in water because that was what Jesus taught his disciples. Essentially, baptism is a part of the plan of salvation according to the teachings of Jesus. Paul was not Jesus. He was only trying to get people to take a step in the right direction toward being a believer in Jesus. Now, run tell that, my sistah!

I still love you, but you sure need to pull your head out of your behind and make sure you understand what you are talking about before you open your mouth … at least when you are talking to me.

From: Dee Dee

To: Monica

Thank you, daughter, for sharing Scripture. Now, Evan, I hope you read the last couple of paragraphs slowly so you can wrap your brain around it. We are to be children of light, not children of darkness. However, as a child of light, if you want to walk in darkness, you have the will to do that, too. And your fellowship with the Lord Jesus Christ will be broken until you start to walk in the light again. Yes, we are free to walk in light and free to walk in darkness. And, as God's child, you will never be able to say, "I could not keep myself from walking in darkness." You see, as a child of God, sin no longer has power over you. God is good like that. If he wanted robots, he would have created them.

Irlean Craven

From: Dee Dee

To: Steve, Evan, and Monica

Evan, everybody does not have to have every sign. Speaking in tongues is just one of many signs, okay? You are almost sounding like the Pharisees and Sadducees, who were just asking questions while trying to catch Jesus disagreeing with Moses.

Soldier

From: Teresa

To: Dee Dee

This is Jesus' prayer for his body. In Acts 2:38, God gave Peter the revelation of what all believers are to do on the day of Pentecost. Remember, Peter was given the keys. If Peter was wrong when he stood up and told everyone to repent and be baptized in the name of Jesus, I believe the other ten would have said, "Peter, you are wrong." That's why Jesus told us to search the Scriptures "for in them you think you have eternal life but these are they which testify of me." Baptism is an outward expression for all believers. Jesus himself was our example.

From: Dee Dee

To: Evan

I never wrote that the disciples did not baptize. I wrote that Jesus never baptized anybody with water before he went to the cross. And, after the cross, he baptized with fire. Can you read the words I am writing? I did not say you were stupid. I said, "Are you stupid?" Shout a while!

From: Dee Dee

To: Evan

Evan, this is not about you. You always think it is about you. Umm! Sad … just sad. Now you have made it personal. Carnality is a trip, uh? It's always there, ready to step in when the word speaks for itself, uh?

Irlean Craven

From: Dee Dee

To: Evan and Monica

I do not read where Jesus said "water" in this verse. Are you adding to the Word? Baptizing by the Holy Spirit is what Jesus brought to the world, okay? There is no sin in being baptized by water, but water baptism does not save or cause you to be born again, bro.

From: Evan

To: Dee Dee

When you called me "stupid," it was about me! Don't try to hide behind what you said now!

Irlean Craven

From: Evan

To: Teresa

Thanks for stating the truth. I wonder if Dee Dee and Steve hear and understand what you have said.

From: Dee Dee

To: Evan and Teresa

Why are you so concerned about me? Shout a while!

Irlean Craven

From: Evan

To: Dee Dee

I said it in the e-mail. I am concerned about you and Steve accepting the truth that is in the Bible. I wonder if you and Steve hear and understand that we are to mock the perfect man, which is Jesus the Christ. If Jesus was baptized, then you need to be baptized, too. Do you get that part? No one is saying that being baptized in water saves you. We all know we are not saved by works. We are saved by God's grace and by following the teachings of Jesus. Now shout a while!

From: Evan

To: Dee Dee

Oh, no! You are not trying to get out of calling me "stupid."

From: Dee Dee

To: Evan

I did not call you stupid. I asked if you were stupid. There is a difference you know. Now run tell that! I still love you, but you did call me stupid! Just repent and ask God to forgive you for being in your flesh and realize we are all saved by grace and, no matter how hard we try, we cannot be perfect in our flesh. We can only be perfect in Jesus. Come on and say "Amen!"

I get it! I was marching to "take me to the water" at the age of eleven, and I was baptized in water. But I was still carnal and marching by Satan's drumbeat. I see nothing wrong with going down in water in Jesus' name. I just have a problem with people saying that water baptism saves, okay?

From: Dee Dee

To: Evan

Again, I asked a question. Who is paying you to be this stupid? I did not call you stupid, okay? You were emailing stupid questions, bro. Shout a while. Again, your interpretation gets you on the wrong track.

Irlean Craven

From: Evan

To: Dee Dee

For the umpteenth time, no one is saying that baptism saves. Your son, Steve, seems to believe he does not need to be baptized because he received the Holy Spirit in his room in Idaho. I was simply imparting to him what the Scriptures say in the Bible as to what the plan of salvation is. If Jesus did it, then we should be found doing it, too. The plan has already been written. Jesus was the perfect man who was our example, not Paul.

An uncle or a cousin or any blood relative in his clan may redeem him. Or if he prospers, he may redeem himself.

Leviticus 25:49

Chapter Two

Uncle Evan, Are You Saved?

Irlean Craven

From: Steve

To: Dee Dee, Evan, and Steve

Uncle Evan ... or is it Pastor? (Please clarify.) Who shall be saved?
If you were to read your Bible and study it, then you would have
quickly taken heed to these passages:

- Matthew 10:22 says, "And ye shall be hated of all men for my
name's sake: but he that endureth to the end shall be saved."

- Matthew 24:13 says, "But he that shall endure unto the end,
the same shall be saved."

- Acts 2:22 says, "And it shall come to pass, that whosoever shall
call on the name of the Lord shall be saved."

- Acts 15:11 says, "But we believe that through the grace of the
Lord Jesus Christ we shall be saved, even as they."

- Romans 10:13 says, "For whosoever shall call upon the name
of the Lord shall be saved."

- John 8:31 says, "Then said Jesus to those Jews which believed
on him, If ye continue in my word, then are ye my disciples indeed."

My next issue has to deal with your responsibilities as a child of God.
Do you know what your responsibilities are? Do you know that you
must obey God's standards? It is not acceptable for a saved person to
continue in his sins. If he does, then it becomes evident that he has
not received the spirit of God or he is intentionally disobeying God.
No matter how many Scriptures you post or reference, I still don't
go along with a saved person hanging out at a liquor store or in strip
clubs. Why? Because that is not his place.

I have more questions, and I need answers immediately because we don't have a lot of time. I know the devil is busy while he stands next to you. I want you to get down on your knees and ask God to deliver you from the suffering. Before you do, I need answers to the following questions with a yes or no only. (Details are not needed).

Are you saved?

1. Have you been baptized by water and the spirit of God?

2. Are you a saint?

3. Are you living according to God's standards?

4. Do you think people claiming to be saved should be permitted to purchase alcoholic beverages from liquor stores?

5. Do you think saved people should participate in the works of the flesh, as outlined in Thessalonians?

6. Are you still letting cares of this world keep your heart away from God?

7. Are you dating?

8. Are you living a lie?

9. Does your past look brighter than your future?

10. Are you really a pastor?

11. Is Jesus your Lord and Savior?

12. Are you letting women usurp authority over you?

13. Do you go to strip clubs?

14. Are you fornicating?

Please answer these questions immediately, but, before you do, get down on your knees and repent. I look forward to your prompt response.

From: Evan

To: Steve

You answer your fifteen questions first. Then I will answer them.

Irlean Craven

From : Dee Dee

To : Steve and Evan

I am hollering now and having a gut laugh. Shout a while! I am one who will buy wine because Jesus made wine. However, I do not get drunk, okay? You know it is for my stomach's sake.

From: Dee Dee

To: Evan and Steve

Hey, bro, answer the questions!

Irlean Craven

From: Macy

To: Evan and Steve

LOL! What in the world! Proverbs 22:1 says, "A sterling reputation is better than striking it rich; a gracious spirit is better than money in the bank."

From: Evan

To: Dee Dee

Now, according to your son, he thinks you should not be drinking wine, liquor, or anything with alcohol in it. According to Steve, if you drink wine or anything with alcohol in it, you are evil. He says it is scriptural. I asked him to show me where it says that, but he has not been able to so far. I am still waiting though. If I am wrong, I want to be right … but only if the Bible says it, not Steve or anyone else.

Irlean Craven

From: Dee Dee

To: Evan

I think in Prov 19 it is written, "Wine is a mocker and strong drink
is a rage and he that drinketh is unwise." It is also written, "Do not
get drunk with wine, but be filled with the Spirit." I cannot find
where we are commanded not to drink wine. Remember we are free
in Christ Jesus. However, we have some family members who are
weak in the faith, and we should not flaunt our strong faith in front
of them. I think that is written in Rom 2. If not, find it for yourself.
We are to be children of light. If we do something that offends our
brother or sister, we should have faith unto ourselves. We might
cause the weak to stumble and fall. The Lord Jesus Christ said that
he would offend some like he did when he made wine. The religious
people called him a winebibber. That's why it is written, "Work
out your own salvation with fear and trembling." Stay out of other
people's struggles while God is working it out in them.

From: Dee Dee

To: Macy, Evan, and Steve

Yes, niece. First, hello. Write about what concerns you the most. Love ya!

Irlean Craven

From: Macy

To: Evan, Steve, and Family

LOL! What in the world! Anywho, I need to write another article. Any suggestions on topics, upcoming events, and so forth?

From: Roger

To: Evan and Monica

First of all, let's stick to the question at all times, or I will pull the plug sooner rather than later. When we read the book of Romans, please make sure we understand that Rom 10:9 was Paul's plea to Israel to accept Jesus as their savior. In Rom 10:3, I believe he called the people ignorant to how salvation comes about because the people were creating their own salvation based on their thoughts. But Paul also told them to not think too highly of themselves. Amen. Now let the conversation begin.

From: Roger

To: Dee Dee

Did we not already have this same conversation when we went to LA? Dee Dee, also in regards to believers being nailed to the cross, now you know that was only something that Jesus could perform. Case in point, you don't even love me that much to die for me. Stop playing and stay in your lane. Smile.

God told us, "Be ye holy; for I am Holy." God also told Peter to set the standards on Earth about how salvation works. It is bound in heaven and on Earth.

From: Roger

To: Steve, Dee Dee, and Evan

That's right. We want answers. In I John 4:1–21, he states to try the Spirit. Stop being fake! It makes no sense to work for a company for twenty years and, when you get ready to cash out and/or retire, find out you never were an employee. That would be sad.

Irlean Craven

From: Dee Dee

To: Roger

Amen! However, you can be saved, know it, and never act like it.
Now that is a problem when it comes to representing. I hear the Lord
Jesus saying, "Why call me Lord Lord and do not as I say?" I think
the Lord Jesus Christ has a problem with carnality.

To all in Rome who are loved by God and called
to be saints: Grace and peace to you from God
our Father and from the Lord Jesus Christ.

Romans 1:7

Chapter Three

Attention, A Saint Is Going Down in Degradation!

Irlean Craven

From: Steve

To: Evan

Wow! It looks like somebody had better let the truth set them f-r-e-e! Uncle Evan, because you wish to address the technicality of baptisms, you have misled yourself down the path of degradation. At the rate you're going, those gasoline drawers you are wearing will be lit before you know it! If you're saved, act like it. If you don't want to act saved, then go grab your bags, call Delta Airlines, and say, "Hi, my name is Suge. I need a one-way ticket to hell!" According to our phone conversation, you are not a saint. Don't make me release the evidence. I'm available for fellowship. Just give me a call!

From: Evan

To: Steve

Steve and Fish, it seems everyone wants to know about Evan. Well, for those who want me to answer Steve's questions, you answer them first. I will be happy to answer them. And no one is living like they should to be saved. We are all saved by grace. If anyone believes differently, please share the Scripture(s) that support your beliefs with the rest of us. I am not trying to debate with anyone. I just want us to find the truth in the Bible.

You are absolutely right. So why don't you answer the questions Steve has asked me? I don't believe I have seen anyone answer Steve's questions, not even Steve. Let us see your light. Go ahead and answer the questions that Steve has asked me. I am interested in reading your answers. It's not because you cannot do it. It's because you don't want us inspecting your life for good reason. The Bible says not to engage in debate and entertain foolishness. This is what Steve is doing. He is bringing foolishness into a simple question of, "Does the plan of salvation include being baptized in water?" The answer is yes.

Steve, on the other hand, wants to deny the Bible and says we should be baptized as part of the process of fulfilling what Jesus said we must do. That is it. That is all. If you want to complain about what I am saying, talk to my boss. His name is Jesus! Also, Steve has the impression that he has to approve of my salvation. This is so crazy and so far from the truth that I had to give him the Scripture on his responsibility is to save himself, not look at other people.

Here is some Scripture for everyone to consider. Remember, all have sinned and fallen short of the glory of God. If any man says he does not sin, he makes God a liar. Let God be true and every man a liar!

Luke 6:42 says, "Either how canst thou say to thy brother, Brother, let me pull out the mote that is in thine eye, when thou thyself beholdest not the beam that is in thine own eye? Thou hypocrite, cast out first the beam out of thine own eye, and then shalt thou see clearly to pull out the mote that is in thy brother's eye."

- Matthew 23:27 says, "Woe unto you, scribes and Pharisees, hypocrites! for ye are like unto whited sepulchres, which indeed appear beautiful outward, but are within full of dead men's bones, and of all uncleanness.

- Luke 16:15–17 says, "And he said unto them, Ye are they which justify yourselves before men; but God knoweth your hearts: for that which is highly esteemed among men is abomination in the sight of God. The law and the prophets were until John: since that time the kingdom of God is preached, and every man presseth into it. And it is easier for heaven and earth to pass, than one tittle of the law to fail."

From: Dee Dee

To: Evan, Steve, and Family

I am tired of you starting a discussion and then giving everybody homework.

Irlean Craven

From: Steve

To: Dee Dee, Evan, and Family

Ha ha!

And so John came, baptizing in the desert region and preaching a baptism of repentance for the forgiveness of sins.

Mark 1:4

Chapter Four

Do You Really Understand?
Even Jesus Commanded
Baptisms

To: Evan

From: Dee Dee

If Steve has enough faith to believe he receives the Holy Spirit, then his confession is true. Now, again, water baptism is symbolic. Yes, Jesus was baptized and stated to John that his baptism was to fulfill prophecy and to suffer it was to be. If you just want to see somebody following in the Lord's footsteps, then you also should be getting ready to be nailed to a cross. Everything the Lord did is not for us to do. What we can do is obey the Lord, like he obeyed his Father God.

From: Evan

To: Dee Dee

Read Mark 16:16–17. "And these signs shall follow them that believe; In my name they shall cast out devils; they shall speak with new tongues." Have you spoken in tongues before? Jesus said these signs will follow those who believe in him. Jesus told everyone to go into all the world and preach the gospel to every creature.

Irlean Craven

From: Evan

To: Family

Everyone, read John 17:8–23. The key verses are: 8, 13, 14, 15, 17, 18, 20, 21, 22, and 23. Let me know what you think.

John 17:8–23 says:

For I have given unto them the words which thou gavest me; and they have received them, and have known surely that I came out from thee, and they have believed that thou didst send me. I pray for them: I pray not for the world, but for them which thou hast given me; for they are thine. And all mine are thine, and thine are mine; and I am glorified in them. And now I am no more in the world, but these are in the world, and I come to thee. Holy Father, keep through thine own name those whom thou hast given me, that they may be one, as we are. While I was with them in the world, I kept them in thy name: those that thou gavest me I have kept, and none of them is lost, but the son of perdition; that the Scripture might be fulfilled. And now come I to thee; and these things I speak in the world, that they might have my joy fulfilled in themselves. I have given them thy word; and the world hath hated them, because they are not of the world, even as I am not of the world. I pray not that thou shouldest take them out of the world, but that thou shouldest keep them from the evil. They are not of the world, even as I am not of the world. Sanctify them through thy truth: thy word is truth. As thou hast sent me into the world, even so have I also sent them into the world. And for their sakes I sanctify myself, that they also might be sanctified through the truth. Neither pray I for these alone, but for them also which shall believe on me through their word; That they all may be one; as thou, Father, art in me, and I in thee, that they also may be one in us: that the world may believe that thou hast sent me. And the glory which thou gavest me I have given them; that they may be one, even as we are one: I in them, and thou in me, that they may be made perfect in one; and that the world may know that thou hast sent me, and hast loved them, as thou hast loved me.

Irlean Craven

From: Monica

To: Family

My understanding of salvation is simple. It is not through water and
it is not the Holy Spirit.Salvation is being saved from the pits of hell.
And in order to do this, you must believe in your heart and confess
with your mouth that God raised Jesus from the dead,And you shall
be saved. Just that simple.Romans 10:9

> Romans 10:9

> That if you confess with your mouth, "Jesus is Lord," and believe
> in your heart that God raised him from the dead, you will be
> saved.Romans 10:8-10 (in Context) Romans 10 (Whole Chapter)

> Romans 10:10

> For it is with your heart that you believe and are justified, and it is
> with your mouth that you confess and are saved.

Not water and not through the acceptance of the holy spirit. The
water baptismis symbolic of who you belong to, not evidence that
you are saved. The HolySpirit is sent to dwell within you after you
have been saved. You cannotreceive the Holy Spirit until after you
have been saved.Salvation is truly between You and God

That's what I believe.

From: Teresa

To: Family

Monica, Auntie is not trying to give you my personal opinion. I am telling you what God's word says. I hope this will help on this discussion. Because my PC is down at home, I cannot chime in. That's why I have to wait until I get to work and check all my e-mails. Love ya.

James was one of the eyewitness of our Lord who walked and talked with him before and after his resurrection. He told us to be the doers of the word and not hearers who only deceive ourselves. Then John, another one of his eyewitnesses, said in Revelation 3:7–8:

> These things saith he that is holy, he that is true, he that hath the key of David, he that openeth and no man shutteth, and shutteth and not man openeth: I know they works behold I have set before thee an open door and not man can shut it: for thou has a little strength and hast kept my word and hast not denied my name.

My question to all who do not believe that water baptism is important. How were your sins washed away? And just like a baby cries when he is born, when did you receive the Holy Spirit? Even the great apostle Paul, after he heard and saw the light while on his way to Damascus to persecute the saints who believed what his eyewitnesses were preaching and teaching, was told by Ananias to repent of sins and be baptized, washing away his sins.

We were all born in sin. There will be no sin in heaven. The only choice you have is to keep them or believe what the words say we all must do. Remember, we are built on the foundation of the apostles and Jesus Christ is the chief cornerstone. Don't you remember that Jesus told Nicomdemus that we must be born of the water and the Spirit? The old man first had to be buried before he could rise and walk in the newness of life. I hope this helps.

From: Evan

To: Teresa

Amen! Amen! Amen! I gave them the Scripture, chapter and verse, regarding what Jesus said about how we must be born again of the water and the Spirit. I gave them the Scriptures, chapter and verse, on what Peter, John, and Jesus said about baptism. Yet they don't study the Bible to get an understanding themselves.

They want to argue that baptism does not save you. No one is saying that baptism saves you. All the Bible says is that baptism was commanded by God through the prophets in the Old Testament, and John the Baptist fulfilled his calling by baptizing people (including Jesus). Jesus then told his disciples to baptize people to follow the command that God had given to him, setting an example for all. Paul was not the one who set the pattern for salvation. God did, and he sent his only begotten son, Jesus, to do that.

What amazes me is that some people don't want to accept what the Bible says. They believe what they believe. They are not going to follow the plan of salvation as it is laid out in the Bible because "being baptized does not save you," according to Steve and Dee Dee. Well, I keep saying that no one said being baptized saves you. It is just part of the plan of salvation. If Jesus had to obey the plan as an example for us, what makes you think God is not requiring you to do the same thing as Jesus did?

Irlean Craven

From: Steve

To: Teresa

Auntie, I like how you said, "The old man first had to be buried before he could rise and walk in the newness of life." This is the very problem I am addressing in regards to the water baptism. You make a valid point when you point out the significance of the water baptism. We all know that, if the water baptism is what makes a person saved, then there is no use for the Bible. Everybody should just go and get dipped.

Again, the issue I am addressing is someone who has been baptized by water and the Spirit instead of someone who has not been baptized by the water, but by the Spirit. According to Uncle Evan, only the first one is saved.

From: Teresa

To: Evan

That is why "one waters, one planteth but God alone give each one of us the increase though the Holy Spirit" if we remember the key is to "rightly divide the word of truth." If not, we will come up with all kinds of theories like everybody else.

Irlean Craven

From: Teresa

To: Steve

You're welcome, Steve.

From: Evan

To: Steve

Now this is how lies get started. Just go ahead and repent for your error in belief. I am waiting for you to send out an e-mail saying you will repent for starting all of this misinformation. I never said that being baptized in water saves you. I am only saying it is part of the plan of salvation. We all know we are saved by grace and Jesus gave us the pattern to follow to put off the old man and put on the new man. Being baptized in water is part of Jesus fulfilling the Scriptures and setting the example for us. It is what God ordained for his new covenant with mankind. Stop tripping and looking at me. Then repent for yourself! This is all about physicality, mentality, and spirituality.

Irlean Craven

From: Monica

To: Teresa

Thank you, Auntie. I appreciate your interpretation. But let me say for the record that I never said that baptism was not important. Never did I say that. I said that it was not required to be saved. This means I am not saved because I was baptized. I am saved only through the confession with my mouth and belief in my heart that God raised Jesus from the dead. Baptism has its purpose. The Bible clearly states what the purpose of water baptism is. Also, in the Bible, it states that, if you have sinned, you need to ask for forgiveness. If water baptism is required to wash away our sins, then we would need to be baptized every day. True?

Also, regarding this verse about Jesus telling Nicodemus he must be born of the water and the Spirit, I explained this in my e-mail to Uncle Evan. My Bible states that being born of water and the Spirit can be understood in various ways:

- It means much the same as "born of the Spirit."

- Water here refers to purification.

- Water refers to baptism that of John or Jesus and his disciples.

- Water refers to physical birth, specifically to the water of the amniotic sac.

From: Evan

To: Monica

Well said. The only thing I was sharing with Steve was the plan includes being baptized in water and the Spirit. These are two separate processes. Jesus, John, and Peter talked about it. Paul said, "Out of the mouth of two or three let every word be established." So, when we read something in the Bible, we need to be careful to understand what has been established and what one person is suggesting.

This is why I asked everyone to provide Scriptures from the Bible (from two or more different people) to support what they believed. I understand what Paul is saying, but can you provide me with another Scripture from someone other than Paul to establish what he said about receiving the Holy Spirit? That is all I am looking for from anyone who can provide it to me.

Irlean Craven

From: Teresa

To: Monica

Thanks so much for the clarity because, as you know, Auntie chimed in late on the subject.

From: Dee Dee

To: Evan

Again, I said the Holy Spirit will bring all nine of the gifts when we are born again. Now, if you need help in praying, then the Holy Spirit will give you the gift of tongues. If you are easily fooled, then he will give you the gift of discernment. You cannot say that, if you do not speak in tongues, then a person is not saved. Paul went over that in the book of Corinthians when he told the church, "I speak in tongues more than ye all."

Irlean Craven

From: Dee Dee

To: Evan, Monica, and Family

First of all, the Lord Jesus Christ fulfilled the plan of salvation. Now we, who are called by his name through the grace of God, have to walk in obedience to the written word by the power of the Holy Spirit. If you do not know the directives given by the Lord Jesus Christ to us, then you cannot obey him. Remember the Lord Jesus Christ came to fulfill the law, not destroy it. Water baptism was a part of the law. That was why he told John to suffer it to be so when John baptized him. Now, under grace, the only baptism that counts is the baptism by the Holy Spirit, which places us into the body of Christ to do the work of the Lord. Water baptism is symbolic. What Peter said on the day of Pentecost was to the Jews.

In Acts 15:28–29, Paul confronted Peter. "How is it that you want to burden the Gentiles with the Law; when we, the Jews, could not handle the Law?" Then Paul, in front of Peter and the rest of the religious leaders, informed the Gentiles that, according to the Holy Spirit, if they would stay away from certain things, they would do well. Now read the chapter for yourself and understand grace and truth came by the Lord Jesus Christ and the law came by Moses. There is nothing wrong with water baptism, but it is symbolic of what happens in our spirit when we are born again of the Spirit. Remember the flesh is not dead. It still wants to do its thing. However, if we follow the Lord Jesus Christ's directives and strengthen our spirit, then we will be lead by our spirit, not our flesh. Now, if you are serious about being a child of light in this evil demonic system, everybody get on your own study for yourself. When I understood the water baptism, I was baptized in water again because I wanted witnesses to see I was not ashamed to be in the family of God. I am still working out my salvation.

From: Evan

To: Dee Dee and Family

Dee Dee, now you want me to be nailed to the cross. Are you sleepy right now? You must be. Listen, I don't want Steve to do anything but understand the Scripture in the Bible. He informed me that he did not know anything about the plan of salvation so I shared the Scripture with him. Unfortunately, we cannot be saved, that is, have the spirit of God, by works. We have to get it through his grace, and the Bible says the evidence of that is speaking in unknown tongues. That is all.

From: Dee Dee

To: Roger, Evan, and Family

The standards Peter made were when God revealed who Jesus Christ was to him. Then the Lord said, "Upon this Rock I will build my church and the gates of hell will not prevail." And what you wrote is also true. I was just making a point to bro number three about following in the steps of the Lord Jesus Christ. When Evan asks a lot of well-known questions, he is usually up to something or trying to put something together.

From: Dee Dee

To: Evan and Family

No, I just want you to know we cannot do everything Jesus did in his physical body.

From: Steve

To: Dee Dee, Evan, and Family

Amen!

Irlean Craven

From: Steve

To: Dee Dee, Evan, Monica, and Family

Uncle Evan, just give up right now. The bottom line is this. If you going to clubs on Saturday night and then show up in the first row of church on Sunday morning, then you are a hypocrite. You only make yourself look worse if you refer to yourself as a saint. I'm sure I'm not the only one who believes this. If you like going to clubs and liquor stores, that's fine with me, but don't tell me that you're a saint.

From: Steve

To: Dee Dee, Evan, and Family

Uncle Evan, again, you are not the one who issues salvation, so you know you gotta fall back on who converses about who is and isn't saved. My whole point is still this. Don't be living a life of degradation all week long and then show up at church on Sunday and talkin' about "Lord forgive me." To be quite honest, if that's what being saved is all about, then you might as well quit readin' your Bible and just make a career out of being a ranked sinner. The issue I am having has to do with true repentance, not the presentation of it. Throw all the Scriptures you want onto these e-mails, but I guarantee you that all the ones you're throwing came from someplace other than your heart.

When you decide to live a life that shows you know how to obey God and not yourself, then you can talk to me about salvation. Because you know so much about the Bible and you believe in it, then you ain't gonna have too many excuses to justify wrong behavior. So I encourage you to continue reading because to whom much is given, much is required. (You do know that, right?) Save the drama for people who can't read.

From: Evan

To: Dee Dee and Family

Dee Dee, so you are going to do and believe what Paul said over what Jesus said? My sister, you do error! Context is very important in reading.

- When Paul said, "I speak in tongues more than ye all," he was dealing with a specific situation. When Jesus said, "These signs shall follow them that believe in me," he was talking about every situation.

- We have multiple religions because people don't want to follow the truth. Jesus never made up any religion. He just spoke the truth.

- If you believe Jesus spoke the truth, then you will keep follow his words. I am not debating or arguing with you on this. I am just giving you the Scripture.

- Again, Paul said, "Follow me as I follow Christ." Paul also said, "Let every word be established by two or three witnesses." So can you give me another witness to what Paul said in Corinthians and any other Scripture you have regarding the plan of salvation? When you respond, make sure you respond with the biblical Scripture in your response. I want to keep this strictly a biblical conversation, not a debate about mine or your ideas. I know how we can be.

From: Evan

To: Dee Dee and Family

Dee Dee, the Bible says, "Let God be true and every man a liar." Did Jesus say you had to be born of the water and of the Spirit to enter into the kingdom of God? Yes! So, if it is not in line with what Jesus said, don't tell me what Paul or anyone else said. This is the problem with a lot of people. They want to put Paul up against Jesus. There is no match. Jesus is the head of the church. He said it, and it is final!

Also, other than Jesus, who do you know who is actually able to be perfect on this Earth, past, present, or future? No one! So don't talk to me about walking in obedience to the written word by the power of the Holy Spirit when you cannot even follow Jesus' instruction on being baptized in his name to fulfill the promise of eternal life of your spirit. So let me stop you right now with the psychobabble about walking in obedience when you cannot even accept what Jesus said about the water baptism.

No, water baptism does not save you by itself, but, if you are going to be obedient to the teachings of Jesus, take your behind down in the water in the name of Jesus and be done with it. This is not a Jewish or Gentile thing. This is a Jesus thing, which makes it a God thing! If you have any questions, talk to my boss. His name is Jesus! All of the rest of your soliloquy is just extra.

Irlean Craven

From: Evan

To: Dee Dee and Family

Let me break this down to you and everyone else so it will forever be broken!

- I ask questions, so I can get answers.

- I ask specific questions so I can get specific answers.

- I like to get others' opinions and facts before I make a decision on what I do or don't believe about a subject matter.

You don't have to wonder why I am asking questions anymore.

From: Evan

To: Dee Dee and Family

Well, Dee Dee, I just want you to know that Jesus said to be baptized in water and the Spirit. Peter confirmed it, and John prophesied about it before it was done. Now shout a while!

Irlean Craven

From: Evan

To: Steve and Family

Steve, you do error. Jesus taught in the synagogues (the churches), and he hung out with the publicans (the sinners). This is what I mean about you. You talk about things you do not know anything about. Don't discuss your bubblegum religion with me. If you don't know the Scriptures from the Bible, then you best fall back off me because all I have for you is these Bible verses. I'll pull one out, and you won't know what hit ya!

From: Evan

To: Steve and Family

Steve, you do error again! Son, you are just fighting the wind. I never said anything about who was saved and who was not. I just asked you one simple question. Have you been baptized in water? When you told me no, I showed you some Scripture in the Bible, which you apparently had never read or paid attention to before, which says we should be baptized in water. John the Baptist said it, Jesus said it, and Peter said it. Now, if you don't like it, call my boss! His name is Jesus, Jesus, Jesus, Jesus, Jesus, Jesus. After you call on him long enough, he will answer you!

Irlean Craven

From: Steve

To: Evan and Family

Well, I'm glad you are finally confessing the truth about this matter. Now, as far as the interpretation of the Bible, I will let the Holy Spirit give me that. You, my brotha, are ranked high among sinners.

From: Steve

To: Evan and Family

Pastor Evan,

Be sure you don't sound like an ear candy preacher who proclaims to be preaching a positive message. Are you excluding the truth found in God's holy word? If you truly love your sheep, you will tell them the truth. God is holy, and he cannot have sin in his presence. Jesus died to redeem us from eternal damnation. This is what the Bible teaches. And this is the very reason why Jesus was around sinners. He wasn't around them because he wanted to do what they did. Read the following every day for your breakfast. I will leave its interpretation for you unto the Holy Spirit.

- Matthew 5:29 says, "And if thy right eye offend thee, pluck it out, and cast it from thee: for it is profitable for thee that one of thy members should perish, and not that thy whole body should be cast into hell."

- Second Timothy 4:2–4 says, "Preach the word; be instant in season, out of season; reprove, rebuke, exhort with all longsuffering and doctrine. For the time will come when they will not endure sound doctrine; but after their own lusts shall they heap to themselves teachers, having itching ears; And they shall turn away their ears from the truth, and shall be turned unto fables."

- Second Timothy 3:12–17, says, "Yea, and all that will live godly in Christ Jesus shall suffer persecution. But evil men and seducers shall wax worse and worse, deceiving, and being deceived. But continue thou in the things which thou hast learned and hast been assured of, knowing of whom thou hast learned them; And that from a child thou hast known the holy Scriptures, which are able to make thee wise unto salvation through faith which is in Christ Jesus. All Scripture is given by inspiration of God, and is profitable for doctrine, for reproof, for correction, for instruction in righteousness: That the man of God may be perfect, thoroughly furnished unto all good works."

- Matthew 7:13–15 says, "Enter ye in at the strait gate: for wide is the gate, and broad is the way, that leadeth to destruction, and many there be which go in thereat: Because strait is the gate, and narrow is the way, which leadeth unto life, and few there be that find it. Beware of false prophets, which come to you in sheep's clothing, but inwardly they are ravening wolves."

I hope this is enough Scripture for ya.

From: Evan

To: Steve and Family

You see how easy it is to accept the truth. Why did it take you so long? As long as you can accept the truth and act on it in a positive way, you will be just fine, and you will encourage others to accept the truth and act on it positively as well.

Irlean Craven

From: Evan

To: Steve and Family

This what happens when Jesus is invoked into the conversation. The enemy has to go, and people who are willing to accept the truth must adopt it for themselves and make it their own. Check out what my nephew Steve did in his e-mail reply below. He took my e-mail and put his name on it! This is what I am talking about. The devil has got to go when Jesus enters into the situation.

From: Evan

To: Steve and Family

Steve, you strain a gnat, but you swallow a camel! First to the things that need to be done according to what Jesus preached and taught. Then we can get philosophical about it. What Jesus said and did while he was on Earth is what we all need to focus on. Let God be true and every man a liar.

Irlean Craven

From: Steve

To: Evan and Family

Uncle Evan, you do error. Jesus taught in the synagogues (the churches), and he hung out with the publicans (the sinners). But Jesus did not participate in their sinful behavior. This is what I mean about you. You talk about thing you do not know anything about. Don't discuss your bubblegum religion with me. If you don't know the Scriptures from the Bible, then you best fall back off me because all I have for you is these Bible verses! I'll pull one out, and you won't know what hit ya!

Life is about spirituality, mentality, and physicality. Start repenting and quit looking at me! You do you, and check with God to make sure you are all right. Quit swerving over into other people's lane! Somebody, come on and say "Amen!"

From: Evan

To: Steve and Family

Steve, we can do this all day and all night, every day and every night, if you want to.

Irlean Craven

From: Evan

To: Steve and Family

Everybody, listen to this! Steve has sent the maximum allowed number of e-mails within a twenty-four hour period, so he cannot mock me anymore today. This is just in case you are wondering why he has not sent e-mail from his hotmail account. God don't like ugly! Because he was mocking me with the word of God, God stopped him. If you ask Steve, he planned to mock me all day long. And look what happened to him.

From: Dee Dee

To: Evan, Steve, and Family

Why do we have to be aware of the Steve and Evan debate? Please, you only need to witness to this discussion. Quit acting like you are on stage with this debate. We are all your audience, Mr. Evan, seventh-born of Laura and Eugene Senior. Chew on that!

Irlean Craven

From: Dee Dee

To: Evan and Family

Remember, all that was before grace!

From: Dee Dee

To: Evan and Family

I am done, my bro. You work it out for yourself, and we all will do the same. Paul wrote the books, and the Holy Spirit approved what he wrote. If you have doubt that Paul was following the Holy Spirit, then I will say, "Let the blind lead the blind." Shout a while!

Irlean Craven

From: Evan

To: Dee Dee and Family

Dee Dee, third-born, my sister in Christ, the answer to your question of why we have to be aware of the Steve and Evan debate is simple. It's because I like to share the gospel. The good news is for everyone. If you know the truth, it shall make you free. But the real question is, "Why do you have to send your e-mails to everyone?"

I don't think I am on stage. I just think I have something important to share when I send information out about specific subject matter, like the water baptism Jesus taught about in the Bible. A famous entertainer once did say, "The world is a stage." Now you chew on that for a while!

From: Evan

To: Dee Dee and Family

Dee Dee, you do error. Peter testified to it after grace and after Jesus had risen from the dead and ascended into heaven. So, for the record, John the Baptist testified to water baptism before Jesus came to be baptized to confirm it. Jesus confirmed water baptism when he said, "You must be born again of the water and of the Spirit." And Peter testified to the water baptism after Jesus was crucified and his disciples received the gift of the Holy Spirit, as Jesus the Comforter taught them about it before he ascended to heaven. Now, repent and accept the truth.

Irlean Craven

From: Evan

To: Dee Dee and Family

Everyone, Dee Dee has just left the building. However, Dee Dee, before you go, you have to be careful to rightly divide the word of God, as Paul wrote. Paul was not the author and finisher of our faith. Jesus is. I would remind you to not focus on Paul. Focus on Jesus the Christ, whom

our faith is based on. If what Paul or anyone else wrote does not line up with what Jesus said, then there is a problem. Somebody, come on and say "Amen!"

From: Dee Dee

To: Evan and Family

Are you on medication again?

Irlean Craven

From: Evan

To: Dee Dee and Family

No, I am not on medication. If I were, I would not be sending e-mails to you.

From: Foxxy

To: Evan and Family

Uncle, just back away from the computer. I think something has gotten a hold of you and your mind. Just slowly go to the Start menu and click Shut Down 'cause you are definitely out of control. Matter of fact, please don't reply to this e-mail. Just back away from the keyboard!

Irlean Craven

From: Evan

To: Foxxy and Family

Hey, Foxxy, you know there is nothing wrong with me. I am simply full of the Holy Ghost, letting your mother and brother know what the Bible really says. They are trying to make stuff up to fit what they believe. It just doesn't work that way with me.

A friend loves at all times, and a brother is born for adversity.

Proverbs 17:17

Chapter Five

What Would Jesus Do (and Spending Time with Your Nephew)

Irlean Craven

From: Evan

To: Family

Steve and Tony, I am sending this e-mail to you two specifically, but everyone else in general. As I work to try to launch my nonprofit company to help the community, families, and children, I realize what my passion really is in life. It is helping people. What I have learned is that, if you cannot help those you love, then you certainly will not help those you don't love. There is an old saying that charity begins at home, which is very true and biblical in principle.

I think I have tried to help my family in many ways. At least I have done what I could. In this regard, I have also learned you can lead a whore to money, but you can't make her think. In other words, I can tell you what to do, but I cannot make you do it. I know your first thought is that Uncle Evan is always in some sort of trouble, but I want you to think about all of the other positive things Uncle Evan is always in, too!

I cannot get you to contribute to the nonprofit, but at least you can spend some time with your own nephew. As for all of the rest of you, you really need to contribute to the nonprofit. The Bible says that if, someone asks you for a coat, then you should give him your cloak, too. If someone asks you to walk with them a mile, then walk with them twain. If someone asks you to help them and you shut up your bowls against him, then you are not of God. Whatsoever you do to the littlest one, you have done to Christ. Now run tell that! When are you going to wake up and put your so-called Christ-like life into action and contribute to the nonprofit I have started for our family and hopefully reach those outside our family as well?

One of those positive things is taking care of Kyle while he is visiting this summer. I am completely ashamed of Tony and Steve for not spending more time with their nephew. I have told them this over and over again. I should not have to send out this e-mail , but, because Steve and Tony have forgotten all of the things they have learned from their uncles, I needed to remind them of the importance of spending time with Kyle and teaching him what it is to be a boy and grow into a young man. Every little bit counts. These are times Kyle will remember for the rest of his life.

Think about it. Do something and stop looking at your Uncle Evan to do everything. I did not teach you to critique me. I think I taught you how to think for yourselves. If you don't know, then now you do. You can do better, so do better!

Irlean Craven

From: Steve

To: Dee Dee and Monica

Uncle Evan? LOL! In fact, I'm LMAO. First of all, you need to quit fronting on these e-mails. I love my nephew. When I am around him, I show him I do that. However, according to you, I am not a man yet because I still live with your sister. Now, Uncle Evan, let's not get into the politics about what Steve and Tony should be doing. Back in 2001, had you not left God's path of righteousness and got on that path of degradation, you would be in a better position to provide for your nephews (Steve, Tony, Pablo, Dennis, Lenny, Adam, Richard, and so on). I have forgiven you for this, but there is no need for you to besmirch my name about things you yourself have problems doing.

On another note, I never called Monica and said I'd take care of Kyle, but I guarantee you that, when I do, I won't be dropping him off at Granny's house like you do. You really need to get a hold of yourself and focus on helping your family and not just trying. I love how you're so quick to identify other people's errors, but you are so quick to omit yours. Last week, I sent an e-mail to you, along with others, asking (not demanding) a moment of your time. Your response to me was none. I called you and spoke with you about this. You told me that you didn't think it was important enough to respond. I humbly took your disrespectful remark and mentally noted that you continued to fall short of the glory of God.

Do not think that, because you can copy and paste biblical Scriptures, you are on another level. Do not think that, because you have creative ideas, you are God's gift to the world. Do not think you are the only person who has a busy schedule. Do not think I am disappointing you. I have now gotten to the point where my expectation of you as my uncle is very low. As of today, I only expect you to look out for yourself and nobody else. I'm completely cool with that. It hurts, but that's what men do, right?

So, while you're sitting at your computer, reading this e-mail, and trying to figure out why I continue to expose your false teachings like this, I want you to look at yourself and Kyle. Then lift up your arms and thank God that Monica is still willing to put her faith in you by believing you will take care of her only son. If you want to help me, then help me. Don't try to run me to floor. If you say you're trying to help the family, then help the family. Don't just try. As a mathematician, a black one at that, my primary focus is to identify problems and solve them. The way I see it, you and Kyle sitting in Uncle Roger's house is not a problem. Or is it? If it is, then you need to explain to us all what the problem is so we can help.

Now do what Jesus said for you to do in your life. Then you'll be all right. I'm ghost.

Irlean Craven

From: Monica

To: Family

I agree with you, Uncle, in this regard. Steve and Tony, you guys should do better if you can. Keep in mind that he is your only nephew, and he is watching you whether you think he is or not. At this point, you guys are his role models. What he sees you doing, he will try to imitate. Would you prefer he imitate women or men? Think about it. Do you have any responsibility?

From: Dee Dee

To: Monica and Evan

As Kyle's grandmother, I already told you, my sons, when I was up there. Make sure you spend time with your nephew. You both are his first uncles. Your Uncle Evan, Roger, and Clive are his grand-uncles. Put on your uncle hats. Go and get him or hang out with him during the week and weekend. Make Mother proud! Shame the devil!

From: Monica

To: Steve and Dee Dee

Wow! It did not need to rise to this level. Steve, you were very eloquent. Your point is well-taken. I just want you all (all of Kyle's uncles, immediate and great) to know it is very important that he is exposed to positive male role models. My whole purpose for Kyle coming to California this summer was so he could see this in action. If this has not or does not happen, not only have I lost time and money, but this experience will have been a waste. I know we all will do the best we can. I appreciate everybody who has extended themselves to show Kyle love and support.

I have no problems with anybody. I know Kyle has grown physically and emotionally. By talking to him, I can tell he has matured. That did not happen with just one person. So, Steve and Tony, I understand you guys are young and doing your thang. I have an idea as to where your focus is, and I understand that. I was twenty-something at one time. So keep doing you and keep it positive. Kyle can learn from that.

Uncle Evan, I am not really sure where all of this is coming from. Is there something you want and are not getting? Regardless, I thank you for extending the offer to spend time with Kyle. He says you are the nicest person in the house. What does that mean? Anyway, taking on this responsibility is great. You didn't have to, but you did. You are not his father, but you stepped up and accepted the challenge. That is what a lot of women want in a man, and I see you are a man of character in this regard. Don't get it twisted. I still think you are misguided on many issues but not in this matter.

Can't we all just get along? Why must we always attack each other and tear everyone down just to make ourselves feel better? I do not understand this. You guys can argue about whatever you want. I just don't want anybody arguing about spending time with Kyle or their lack thereof. Whatever! Just do what you can. In just little over a month, Kyle has already bonded with everybody and enjoys spending time with everybody. (Actually, he says he likes going over to Auntie Teresa's and Granny's house, but Uncle Evan's and Uncle's Roger house is not so fun.) I am sure this is because these are men and he is being exposed to stuff he wouldn't normally be exposed to. Whatever his reasoning is, he will get over it. As far as I am concerned (and my concern is only for Kyle), he is doing fine with whatever is going on.

Irlean Craven

From: Evan

To: Steve and Family

If you want to know some of the blessings God has already done for the nonprofit, just ask Tony. He has been participating as much as he can. He can tell you the response from those outside of the family from at least one meeting he attended with me.

The e-mail I sent is not about me waiting for the family to do something to help the nonprofit. It is to tell the family they are not acting Christ-like regarding the nonprofit. The nonprofit is all about doing exactly what I am doing with Kyle. I hope this clears up your mind.

From: Teresa

To: Monica

Now let me address the nonprofit. It appears that, when the Lord gives any of us an idea, vision, or dream, we as a family love to share it with the family. However, I believe the one who had the dream, idea, or vision must take sole procession of it and not look to the family to fulfill it. It's like Joseph, who dreamed a dream and got so frustrated because his family did not support him. It later turned out to be one of the biggest nonprofit businesses of the world.

In my understanding of the way God works, he often lays a great responsibility on one person through dreams and visions, but the details of how the dream or vision plays out is totally up to God. We must remember Joseph, whose family rejected his dream but did not cause his dream to die.

When the Lord places something in our heart so strong, his word tells us "not to despise small beginnings … for in due season you shall reap if you faint not." Evan, if it appears that you are not receiving the support you expected from your family at this time, it is possible that you are focusing on the set of people to fulfill your dream. I just want to encourage you that God has a vast harvest out there awaiting you, but, for now, your job is to keep the faith because this nonprofit business will be bigger than you and our family. If you will allow me to have a little folly, maybe it will take you to be thrown into the pit before you move to where the Lord will use you to be a blessing. In the meantime, the right attitude to have at this time is, "Lord, help me to be a blessing, not bless somebody to bless me."

Now, regarding Kyle, I agree it is very important for all the male uncles and cousins to spend as much time with him as possible because he will be leaving soon and going back home to North Carolina. He can only share with his family the time that each one of us spends with him. So, when he gets back home and never mentions your name to his mom, aunties, and cousins, all I can say is, "Shame on you."

From: Steve

To: Evan

What exactly are you doing with Kyle? I hope it's not dropping him off because that would be equivalent to you dropping off your nonprofit. Tsk! Tsk! Tsk! I'll be calling you later today to make sure you're still holding on to God's unchanging hands.

From: Evan

To: Steve and Family

The things I am teaching Kyle:

1. I am teaching him how to be a boy.

2. I am teaching him how to think and act like a little boy.

3. I am teaching him how to throw a ball and catch a ball correctly.

4. I am teaching him how to run correctly.

5. I am teaching him how not to scream like a little girl.

6. I am teaching him how not to act like a little girl.

7. I am teaching him how to sit and listen to the word of God in church.

8. I am teaching him how to clean up after himself.

9. I am teaching him how to fold his own clothes after they are washed.

10. I am teaching him how to run correctly.

11. I am teaching him how to act around men versus women.

12. I am taking him around other boys his age so he can learn how to play with other boys.

13. I am teaching him how to stay out of grown folks' business.

14. I am teaching him how men are different from women so he shouldn't expect men to treat him like women do.

15. I am teaching him to help his mother around the house when he gets back home.

16. I am teaching him how to wash the dishes.

17. I am teaching him how to wash out the bathtub after he takes a bath.

18. Etc.

Irlean Craven

From: Foxxy

To: Evan, Steve, and Family

Very interesting, Uncle. Can you please give us a visual of Kyle
washing dishes? I need to have this recorded in my memory.

From: Dee Dee

To: Foxxy

Now, Foxxy, I agree we need to see pictures of this. Roger, when you get home, take pictures of the clean house and kitchen, please.

Irlean Craven

From: Evan

To: Dee Dee and Family

I tell you what. If you all send me pictures of your clean house, I will send you pictures of this clean house! Well, can I get an "Amen"?

From: Steve

To: Evan

Why stop at eighteen things? I need a list of all thirty-six things you are teaching. I think two and three are the same things and so is five and six. Eight and nine are very similar. With this being said, all I can say is, "Job well done!" I look forward to making sure my nephew has been transformed into the new creature you've molded him to be. Now let the church say, "Amen! Amen! Amen! Thank God for the Holy Ghost!"

Do not provoke or irritate or fret your children, lest they become discouraged and sullen and morose and feel inferior and frustrated.

Colossians 3:21

Chapter Six

Confrontation at the Wrong Time

Irlean Craven

From: Dee Dee

To: Foxxy, Tracy, and Monica

Good morning, my daughters. I'm just getting around to e-mailing
you this message concerning your children and my relationship. I
don't know if Tracy told you both about the dialogue she and I had
concerning how she is raising her daughter. If not, I won't go into it
either. Now it appears that Stacy has been telling her mother things
in confidence about why she doesn't want to stay with me, along with
the other complaints she has with me. Well, I just want to tell all of
you this now so I don't have to go through this again. If your children
come to you with a complaint about me, please do not partner with
them by justifying their complaints. Please tell them to bring their
complaints to me. Also, if you ever see or hear me speaking to your
children and feel I am saying something wrong, please wait until I
am finished. Then come to me in private and inform me of it. If you
choose to step to me in front of your children, then it will be on you
all. I am your mother.

I raised you. I am not trying to raise your children. So, if I tell them
something they are doing is a concern to me, I expect you all to tell
them to not do those things around me. You all know me better than
they do. I am saying this because I gave Tracy a pass when she was in
California. She stepped to me in front of Stacy concerning the red
polish on her toes. I also gave Tracy a pass because John was her guest
in Granny's house.

Please do not let your children to manipulate you by allowing
them to speak against your mother just because I won't let them do
what they want around me. Your job as parents is to raise them to

understand they are the children, not your partners. Tracy, if Stacy ever comes to you again and tells you she is having a problem with me, her grandmother, I hope you will be parent enough to tell her to come to talk to me. If she chooses not to speak to me about it, then you should keep it to yourself. It concerns me that you allow her to confide in you the things that bothers her. Exposing it during a moment of dialogue between Stacy and me is very immature on your part. You are her parent.

In closing, please understand me when I say this, daughters. Your children are your children. You are my children. That is enough for me. I do not want your children around me if they do not want to be around me. I was born without them. I can live without them if they are having a hard time with me being their grandmother.

Please explain this to them so I won't have to. But, if you don't explain it to them, I will. I do not want to see color on their toes or nails until they are sixteen years old, please. If I see them with color on their toes and nails, then I will confront them every time. So, because I do not live around them, just tell them to respect my wishes when I come around them.

I just wanted to make sure I informed you all concerning this issue. There will be no passes if I am confronted by any of you in front of your children about things I told them not to do around me. Make sure you inform their daddies so, if they have anything to say, they can say it to me now.

Irlean Craven

From: Tracy

To: Dee Dee, Foxxy, and Monica

Mother, thanks for the pass. That means God gave you one as well. Please know that what you do to me, you do to my Father. I am in Christ Jesus. So, if you want to continue, let Satan trick you and deceive you. Carry on!

As for my child, if you do not want to see polish on her, then I suppose it's best that we see you in two years. I am not going to allow you to rule and reign over my household. You never permitted anyone to rule and reign over yours. Your demands will not govern me or my child. I suppose your demands give you some type of power, but it is not of God. That spirit will not go around regulating things, at least not here.

As for my daughter, you can speak to her and tell her how you feel. But, if you don't do it with the help of God, you are only destroying the relationship between you. If it means more that you get your way in this life than to walk in the love described in I Cor 3, then carry on!

The Bible puts it like this. Please note that I'm just trying to make this plain and simple as possible. The King James Version still bears witness.

I Cor 13:1–7 says:

If I speak with human eloquence and angelic ecstasy but don't love, I'm nothing but the creaking of a rusty gate. If I speak God's Word with power, revealing all his mysteries and making everything plain as day, and if I have faith that says to a mountain, "Jump," and it jumps, but I don't love, I'm nothing. If I give everything I own to the poor and even go to the stake to be burned as a martyr, but I don't love, I've gotten nowhere.

So, no matter what I say, believe, and do, I'm bankrupt without love. Love never gives up. Love cares more for others than for self. Love doesn't want what it doesn't have. Love doesn't strut. Love doesn't have a swelled head. Love doesn't force itself on others. Love isn't always "me first." Love doesn't fly off the handle. Love doesn't keep score of the sins of others. Love doesn't revel when others grovel. Love takes pleasure in the flowering of truth. Love puts up with anything. Love trusts God always. Love always looks for the best. Love never looks back, but keeps going to the end.

So my concern, after reading what love is, is that you continue to enforce what you want and what you say. This is not of God, and that spirit has no power here.

From: Dee Dee

To: Tracy, Foxxy, and Monica

To my first-born daughter (and not my only daughter), God did not give me a pass. I did not need one. I am not on your level. I gave birth to you. You did not give birth to me. You are an adult just like me, and I expect you to act like one. It is not written in the Bible that what I do to you or anybody else I do to my Heavenly Father. Your response to my e-mail reminds me of a Scripture. "Thinking yourself wise, you speak like a fool."

So I will say from my perspective that you are so religious when it comes to the word of God that you think the scriptures are talking about you, not our Lord and Savior, Jesus Christ. You often praise satan by using a capital "S" in this e-mail. I am not sure why you always bring satan up in everything and everybody, including me. But you should know by now that it is written, "All power in heaven and earth is given to my Lord and Savior Jesus Christ."

I am not trying to rule over your house or your daughter. I said I didn't want to see color on her toes or fingers. So go back and read what I wrote. I don't ever have to see you or your child in this life if God permits. It isn't that serious. I don't live with you. Now that I know how angry you are as my daughter, I will pray the Lord Jesus Christ will touch your mind and remind you of what your position is in this world.

If you think it is to be in conflict with me, then do what you do. You are just showing yourself and the world why the Lord Jesus Christ had to bring salvation to the "whosoever will." If you were in Christ, then you would be in peace with God 24-7. Your response to this e-mail says you are a very troubled child living in an adult body and playing a victim role when it comes to your childhood. Sad! You are a parent. Act like one. You are a disappointment to me as your mother when it comes to you being able to parent your own child.

You want to use Scripture to convince your daughter not to follow one directive from me? Then, if you like it, I love it. I don't have to see her after two years either if it makes you feel more powerful. All I can say is that, one day, she will be an adult. That is when you and the world will see your report card regarding your parenting skills. Because you sound like a victim, I will assume you are raising a victim, too. You may have been victimized like everybody else on the planet, but you don't have to be a victim unless you choose to. The fact you still know who you are today means you have survived whatever negative came against you as a child or adult. So stop acting and sounding like a victim.

I have already spoken to your daughter about my request. I just wanted you to know that, the next time you step outside your land and try to step to me in front of her, she will have a Kodak moment for life concerning how a daughter should address her mother when she sees her mother saying something she does not agree with concerning her child. Do I make this clear to you, daughter? I am not against you voicing your opinion. I am against any of my children starting with you trying to step to me at the wrong time.

Remember that! Nobody loves your child more than you do. However, you will need more than your child one day. So make sure you are raising her to be a survivor, not a victim, when it comes to me.

The only love I have for you and the rest of the world is the love of God, my daughter. Your problem is that you think God's love always feel good. If you are going to fight for your daughter, then make sure it is over something more important than nail polish.

From: Tracy

To: Dee Dee, Foxxy, and Monica

Mother, I forgive you for your offenses, and I'm praying for you. The Lord is my vindicator, and he will fight for me. This battle is not mine, but it is the Lord's. I love you and pray nothing but good comes your way. I appreciate all you have done for me. May the Lord reward you for your good. No Kodak moments will be taken with me for I am not ignorant of Satan's devices. The Bible prepares us in Eph 6:10 to put on the whole armor so we may be able to stand against the wiles of the devil.

The armor required here is in Eph 6:15. "And having shod your feet with the preparation of the gospel of peace." Remember that God wants us to "pursue peace with all people, and holiness, without which no one will see the Lord."

By the way, Satan is capitalized all over the Bible. Jesus' comments in the Bible in reference to him also begin with a capital letter. It's probably no different than me addressing you because it is your name. Names, subjects, title, and the like should begin with a capital letter. No praise whatsoever was intended for the enemy. See Matt 16:23 for an example.

From: Dee Dee

To: Tracy, Foxxy, and Monica

I am glad to know that you are a forgiving person, but I need to know what you are forgiving me for. The Lord Jesus Christ will fight for you? Where is that written, daughter? I would like to be educated. Yes, the battle is the Lord's. But do you know what that battle is?

If I remember correctly the Bible says in Gal 5:19 that those are our battle to fight against. In Gal 5:22, it is our victory if we bring forth the fruits of the Holy Spirit. We have other personal battles that the Lord Jesus gave us the victory over if we will follow his directives.

It is written, "Put on the whole armor of God so that we will be able to stand." This is another personal battle we must fight, not God. So what battle are you talking about that God will fight for you? Remember, it is written, "In all your getting, get understanding." That is another personal battle for you to fight, not God. There are so many more personal battles, but I will stop with these few.

The Lord Jesus Christ already vindicated those of us in the body of Christ when he died and rose again. He is now seated on the right hand of our Father. So, again, what are you talking about? This dialogue is about Tracy and Monica not confronting me in front of their children when they do not agree with what I am saying to their children. Nothing more. But Tracy and Monica wanted to bring up their childhood issues to justify themselves when confronting me, their mother, in front of their children. You are right. There will not be any Kodak moments if you do not confront me in front of your child. However, if you fail to control your mouth, which is a member, there will be a Kodak moment. Remember that the power of life and death is in the power of the tongue.

Irlean Craven

From: Tracy

To: Dee Dee, Foxxy, and Monica

The Lord will deal with you concerning me! You'll see. Unfortunately, I would love to educate you, but I must resort to your favorite Scripture concerning teaching. "But the anointing which ye have received of him abideth in you, and ye need not that any man teach you: but as the same anointing teacheth you of all things, and is truth, and is no lie, and even as it hath taught you, ye shall abide in him."

By the way, you are forgiving among many things, but the most recent is lying on me. "You often praise satan by using a capital 'S' in this e-mail."

From: Dee Dee

To: Tracy, Foxxy, and Monica

I do not need you to forgive me for anything, so, unless I ask you to forgive me, do not tell me you forgive me. The key words are "You do not have to tell me." It is my perspective only concerning the capital "S." It is not written anywhere in the Bible, Tracy. So how can you say my perspective is lying on you? Just continue to talk about everything else and not focus on my request of "not confronting me while I am talking to your child." I want to make sure Tracy and Monica understand, like Foxxy. I want you both to know what I am saying and why I am saying it. Therefore, all I want to hear from Tracy and Monica is, "Yes, I understand what you are saying, but I will confront you in front of my daughter anyway." Then the dialogue will end.

Irlean Craven

From: Foxxy

To: Dee Dee, Tracy, and Monica

Hmmm, Mother, what exactly do I understand? Just curious. I've been chillin' in the cut. Oh, when I said I understood where you are coming from, I think we understand where you are coming from, but don't necessarily agree. It's sorta like we understand what happened with Juanita, but we don't agree with what happened.

From: Dee Dee

To: Foxxy, Tracy, and Monica

Foxxy, your response to my first e-mail was, "What is going on? Where is the love?" Now I do not believe you are talking about my first e-mail. I believe you were talking about your sister's response to my first e-mail. You did not assume I was trying to run your house and raise your child. You ask me to consider my relationship with my mother's request when it came to my children. I responded, and you have been silent until now. So, by your silence, I assumed you understood what and why I was saying what I was saying. Now, if you do not understand, then I will say it again:

> Do not confront me in front of your children if you feel I am saying something wrong. Wait until I am done. Then come to me in private. Then I can correct myself with your child. I do not want to be arguing in front of my grandchildren with my children.

However, if my children want it that way, then that is the Kodak moment your children will have. If this is about a power struggle for you all, then, the next time I confront your children about anything, just step to me in front of them.

Irlean Craven

From: Foxxy

To: Dee Dee, Tracy, and Monica

Why are you yelling?

From: Dee Dee

To: Foxxy, Tracy, and Monica

I am tired of repeating myself to my adult children who have children. I am just asking for common sense when there is a dialogue going on between two people, not just when I am talking to my grandchildren. When I am not around and you all want them to walk around with their butts out, that is your business. I am talking about what I do not want to see on them when I am around. As long as you all know, I will be confronting your children about the nail polish. Your children know I will be confronting them. Then do not act like that when I am confronting them. You do not have to jump in to defend them. If you do, you will give them a Kodak moment for life. Now you have been warned. The ball is in your court. Your children are all old enough to make the call for themselves. And if they think you can protect them from me confronting them, then they are deceived like you are, my daughters. December can be the last time I visit you all or see you all if that is what you want. I did not raise children to argue or fight with them in front of my grandchildren. That is just too ghetto.

Irlean Craven

From: Foxxy

To: Dee Dee, Tracy, and Monica

This is quite bizarre, and I don't get it. You have seen all your grandkids with fingernail polish on at one time or another. I don't understand why you are attacking us on this particular issue. This doesn't seem to be a battle worth fighting. What was the final outcome in California? Stacy got to keep her fingernail polish on because her parents said it was okay. We know you like to be in control. It's probably scary for you not to be, but maybe you should just trust God on this issue instead of alienating and threatening everyone with a special Kodak moment. Maybe you should be Kodak's spokeswoman, but I digress.

When you are going to meet your Maker, are you going to look back and think, "My granddaughters shouldn't have worn that red polish!" I think there are bigger issues we need to focus on, like how are we going to win more souls to the kingdom of God instead of how we're going to run Revlon out of business.

From: Dee Dee

To: Foxxy, Tracy, and Monica

Foxxy, it is not about just fingernail polish. It is about dark colored polish before they are sixteen. Is this so hard to understand? Did you answer the three questions I e-mailed you all yesterday concerning how many predators live in you zip code and what the dark colors mean to them?

Irlean Craven

From: Monica

To: Dee Dee, Foxxy, and Tracy

This is really the last comment I will make on this issue. Are you for real? I really don't think you get it, and that is what is so frustrating about you. Whether you are right or not, it really does not matter to you. Does it? I get it. It's about what have I said. If you don't comply, then you suffer the consequence for your actions. Do you not see the control factor here? You are always so ready to cut people off, like you don't need anybody. You keep emphasizing the fact that you have many daughters and one less will make no difference to you. Do you realize that you are getting old? Why are you destroying personal relationships between your children for the sake of having your way? It is not worth it. You keep talking about Kodak moments, suffering consequences, and the such. Is this your last-ditch effort to remain in control? Well, it isn't working. Our will is as equally as strong as yours.

When is the last time you actually got into a fight with anybody? Do you not realize that you are almost sixty years old and threatening to engage in an altercation with your spry daughters? You have to be totally delusional. Do you really think you are twenty years old? Maybe you will get your equalizer and equalize the situation. You know how you do. Whatever. Your threats have no weight here. The only person you stand to hurt is yourself. At the end of the day, will you be okay if none of your children have any relationship with you? Is it really worth it to you? You do not need to be in control of everybody and everything. I know it's hard for you because you been this way for a very long time.

Everybody cannot be wrong about you. This is so not about fingernail polish. It is about control and your lack of it. I know that has got to be a humbling realization, and you are fighting it every step of the way. I commend you for the fight. You are a true fighter. If fighting keeps you young, then understand why you do it, but do not be disappointed when you do not get the results you intended. Just continue to stay young at heart. Please don't give up your fire. It makes you who you are, but don't ask us to give up our fire either.

Finally, I do not care what you say or what you do. I will always be your second daughter, and I will always love you. You cannot change that. You can disown me, stop talking to me, or possibly even kill me, but, ultimately, you will be the one who has to stand before our Heavenly Father. Will all the things you've done to destroy your relationships be worth it in the end? Just know one thing about your second-born daughter. I am a child of God. In the end, I will receive my reward from my Father, who is in heaven. You have nothing that tops that reward. Please, I no longer want to comment because I believe that, in some sadistic way, you are enjoying this.

Irlean Craven

From: Foxxy

To: Monica, Dee Dee, and Tracy

Mother, you keep saying we are not allowed to confront you. Are we allowed to quote Scripture to you in front of your grandchildren?

From: Dee Dee

To: Foxxy, Monica, and Tracy

My third-born daughter, I am again saying you can quote as much Scripture to me as you want. You can confront me as much as you want. I am requesting that you all do not confront me while I am confronting your children about something I told them not to do in front of me. I cannot say it any clearer. If you feel you want to fight me on this request because you know me better than they do, then just confront me. I failed to teach you this as children. Parents never argue with their children in front of their grandchildren concerning the grandchildren. It is to prevent emotional confusion for the grandchildren. When grandchildren see their parents arguing with their grandparents concerning them, they will feel like they have to choose a side or they caused the argument. Is that what you all want for your children? If so, if you like it, I love it.

Irlean Craven

From: Foxxy

To: Dee Dee

I'm just trying to understand if you consider us quoting Scripture to you as a confrontation? Can I use an example? Let's say a child named Sarah has on red fingernail polish that her parents said it was okay for her to wear. Then Grandma Wendy had an issue with it and told Sarah not to wear it. Is Grandma Wendy causing Sarah, a child, to disobey her parents? Shouldn't Sarah honor her mother and father, as the Bible said, or listen to Grandma Wendy?

From: Dee Dee

To: Foxxy and Dee Dee

No! Quoting Scripture can be confrontational, but you have my permission to confront me using the Scriptures. Now to answer your question. If her grandmother told her not to wear it and the child is old enough to make her own decisions, then that child should follow her own mind to make life easier on herself. If that child is a baby, then her grandmother should not say anything to the child at all. Her grandmother should speak to the parents about her concerns only.

If the child is old enough to make life easier on herself, then she should not let her grandmother see it on her when her grandmother is around. Her parents are not commanding her to wear red polish, right? The child has a choice, right? If the child is smart, she can have the best of both worlds. If the child is feeling victimized by her parents and grandmother, then the child is emotionally unstable. So, to answer your question, her grandmother is not causing the child to disobey her parents. Remember the parents said the child could wear red polish. They did not say the child had to wear red polish. The child has freedom of choice with her parents. If the child chooses not to wear red polish, she is not disobeying her parents. If the child chooses to wear red, she must at least expect grandmother to confront her on it.

www.ingramcontent.com/pod-product-compliance
Lightning Source LLC
Chambersburg PA
CBHW051251280526
45784CB00002B/719